D1602195

The Last Bright Days

The Last Bright Days

A Young Woman's Life in a Lithuanian Shtetl on the Eve of the Holocaust

Edited By

Frank Buonagurio

Jewish Heritage

YIVO

Institute for Jewish Research

Copyright © 2011 by Frank Buonagurio

All rights reserved. This book or any portion thereof may not be reproduced or used in any manner whatsoever without the express written permission of the publisher except for the use of brief quotations in a book review.

Co-published by Jewish Heritage, New York, and YIVO Institute for Jewish Research, New York

Printed in China

First Printing, 2011

Publisher's Cataloging-In-Publication Data

The last bright days : a young woman's life in a Lithuanian shtetl on the eve of
  the Holocaust / edited by Frank Buonagurio ; [journals and photographs by
  Beile Delechky ... et al.].

   p. : ill., maps, col. facsims. ; cm.

   The journals of Beile Delechky were translated into English from the original Yiddish.
   ISBN: 978-0-9677697-9-0

   1. Kavarskas (Lithuania)--Social life and customs--20th century--Pictorial works. 2. Delechky,
Beile--Family--Pictorial works. 3. Jewish women--Lithuania--Kavarskas--20th century--Diaries. 4.
Women immigrants--United States--20th century--Diaries. 5. Delechky, Beile--Diaries. I. Buonagurio,
Frank. II. Delechky, Beile.

DS135.L52 K28 2011
947.93/0841   2011924507

www.jewishheritageproject.org

www.yivo.org

There is an intrinsic fascination with old photographs. They are our way of looking back in time. When we see people staring, unsmiling, back at us across the years, we wonder what their lives were like. We wonder what became of these people with their antiquated clothes and hairstyles. What were the stories of their lives?

The story of the people in the photographs in *The Last Bright Days* includes a tragic role in the Holocaust. But these people were also part of another story. They lived in a community where they practiced their religion, went to school and to work, enjoyed the companionship of friends and the love and support of their families. It is a story that we have in common, a story that comes to us across time and geography and stands against the bigotry that denied the Jews of Lithuania their humanity.

The photographs of *The Last Bright Days* belonged to Beile Delechky. She brought with her to America hundreds of photographs of the people and places of her youth. She and her brother Moishe had been the town photographers in Kavarsk, Lithuania.

In November of 1938, Beile took a bus west, leaving behind her home, her family, her friends and the town of Kavarsk where she had grown up. That bus took her to Kaunas, the capital of Lithuania, and to a train that brought her through Poland and Nazi Germany to Rotterdam, Holland. In Rotterdam, she boarded the ocean liner, Veendam, and sailed for the safety of her relatives in America.

Nearly all that Beile left behind in 1938 would never be seen again. In June of 1941, the Second World War and the Holocaust swept over Lithuania and the town of Kavarsk. Of her immediate family, only Beile's sisters, Minna, who remained in Lithuania, and Raisel, who had emigrated to Argentina, survived. Memories and photographs were all that remained of what had been the vital Jewish community of Kavarsk.

The photos in this book are only a sample of Beile's collection, a small reminder of all that existed and was lost. Though the people depicted were a part of the tragedy of the Holocaust, they were also part of that other story, the story that we all share. These photos are presented not simply to memorialize their tragic deaths but also as a reminder of the lives they lived.

A number of the photographs in this book are accompanied by Beile's poems and excerpts from the more than two dozen notebooks and diaries she brought with her to America.

You will see the name Deliackaite on Beile's documents in this book. That is the Lithuanian version of the family name with the ending 'aite' used for unmarried women. For the family in general, I have chosen to use the Slavic version of the name, Delechky.

It is unfortunately impossible to accurately credit all the photos in this book. Some were taken by Beile, others by her friend Feigeh, who was town photographer before her. Some appear to be studio portraits.

In preparing the photographs for this book, I digitally repaired the most serious damage and made adjustments where necessary to improve clarity.

Frank Buonagurio

LITVAKS:
Introduction to The Last Bright Days: A Young Woman's Life in a Lithuanian Shtetl on the Eve of the Holocaust

The photographs that Beile Delechky brought with her when she left Europe for the United States in 1938 belong to the shattered legacy of Lithuania's small-town Jews between the two world wars. The term "shtetl" too often conjures up "Fiddler on the Roof" stereotypes of pious Jews mired in a folkloric past. These pictures from the hamlet of Kavarsk (Kavarskas, in Lithuanian), many of them taken by Beile herself, unselfconsciously reveal a more nuanced view of everyday reality for Jews and Lithuanians during the 1930s.

Lithuanian Jews, whether they hailed from Lithuania proper or from neighboring Belarus and northeastern Poland, were known throughout Eastern Europe as Litvaks. The stereotypical Litvak combined rigorous adherence to tradition with a hyper-commitment to rationalism and resistance to mystical strains of Judaism. Lithuania was especially fertile ground for the cultural, political and social movements that transformed Jewish life in the nineteenth and twentieth centuries. It was the heartland of both the Zionist and the Jewish labor movements, and it was an important test-bed for experiments in Jewish communal and cultural autonomy. Lithuanian Jews proudly embraced their Litvak identity.

Kavarsk was a typical Lithuanian market town and as such it offers a microcosm of Jewish life in that country. Lithuania was an overwhelmingly rural and agrarian country, its economy heavily reliant upon trade in grain and timber. The interwar decades posed dire economic and political challenges. The newly established Lithuanian republic was cut off from its economic hinterland in the former Russian empire (by then the Soviet Union) and was cut off as well from neighboring Poland, which had incorporated Lithuania's historic capital of Vilnius (Vilna, Wilno) within its boundaries. From 1926 until 1939, Lithuania was to all intents and purposes a dictatorship, threatened moreover by the external forces that eventually plunged the country into war and deprived it of its independence. These factors weighed heavily upon the country's Jews and encouraged the emigration of many of them during those decades to destinations overseas, especially to South Africa – but also to Palestine, South America, and the United States.

Nevertheless, during the brief interlude between the two world wars, the Jewish communities of independent Lithuania exercised a considerable degree of autonomy. *The Last Bright Days* includes photographs of the Folks-shul, the Jewish elementary school – an institution that was emblematic of the Jews' recognized status as a national minority. Directly or indirectly, other photographs also reveal the political engagement of Beile Delechky's contemporaries in Kavarsk, be it through their involvement with Zionist groups or in the Communist loyalties of Beile's sister, Minna.

Clothing styles along with other sartorial details serve as reminders that Kavarsk was not frozen in amber; indeed, the young people in these photographs would not have stood out at all elsewhere in 1930s Europe. Under normal circumstances, they would doubtless have achieved many of their aspirations for a better life and a better world; the times, however, were anything but tranquil. Beile Delechy's photographs are thus all the more valuable for having captured a moment in the history of a civilization that was soon to be irretrievably extinguished.

Zachary M. Baker
Reinhard Family Curator of Judaica and Hebraica Collections
Stanford University Libraries

Acknowledgements

Among the many people who have provided generous support and kind encouragement in the production of *The Last Bright Days*, I would like to especially thank the following:

Ken Blady who translated Beile's Yiddish poems, diaries, notebooks and the Yiddish inscriptions found on the backs of many of the photographs. Ken was the first to urge me to seek a wider audience for Beile's photographs and writings.

Raphael Susnowitz, Beile's son, who provided much material including Beile's notebooks and journals and support in their translation.

For their generous contributions to and abiding interest in this project:
Donald Buonagurio, Karen Bottar and Nora Buonagurio
David Garcia and Karen Maestas
Nick Lawrence and Joyce Zolkiewicz
Peggy Niswander
Yasuyo Satoh
John and Stacey Singer
Dennis Tsai and Gerri Donato
Ray and Shirley Watson
George and Linda Wertheim

Diane and Leighton Siegel for permission to use the story of Michel Labe Segal from the Siegel Family History.

Ralph Jaffe's fascinating memoir, *The Shtetl That Was*, provided details of life in Kavarsk.

Alan Adelson, Executive Director of Jewish Heritage, for his patience with my many questions, for his expert guidance and his many hours of effort on behalf of *The Last Bright Days*.

And as always, my wife Carol, Beile's daughter, for her sage advice throughout.

NORWAY

SWEDEN

Helsinki

Tallinn

ESTONIA

NORTH SEA

DENMARK

BALTIC SEA

LATVIA

Riga

Moscow

Volga

Oka

LITHUANIA

Kavarsk

Kaunas

Wilno
(Vilna)

SOVIET

RUSSIAN

Vitebsk

Smolensk

S F S R

Königsberg

DANZIG

POMERANIA

GERMANY

Elbe

GERMANY

Minsk

BELORUSSIAN
SSR

UNION

Poznań

Płock

W. Bug

Warsaw

Łódź

POLAND

Wrocław

Lublin

Chernigov

(U S S R)

SILESIA

Vistula

Chełm

Łuck

Zhitomir

Kiev

Katowice

PRAGUE

BOHEMIA

MORAVIA

Kraków

Przemyśl

Lwów

Dnieper

CZECHOSLOVAKIA

Danube

Brno

Bratislava

SLOVAKIA

SUBCARPATHIAN RUS

Stanisławów

U K R A I N I A N

S S R

S. Bug

AUSTRIA

Budapest

Debrecen

SWITZER-
LAND

HUNGARY

Cluj

MOLDAVIA

Dniester

BESSARABIA

Chișinău
(Kishinev)

Odessa

TRANSYLVANIA

Timișoara

Sibiu

ROMANIA

ADRIATIC SEA

YUGOSLAVIA

WALACHIA

Bucharest

Danube

DOBRUJA

BLACK   SEA

ITALY

BULGARIA

0   100   200 miles

0   100
   200 km

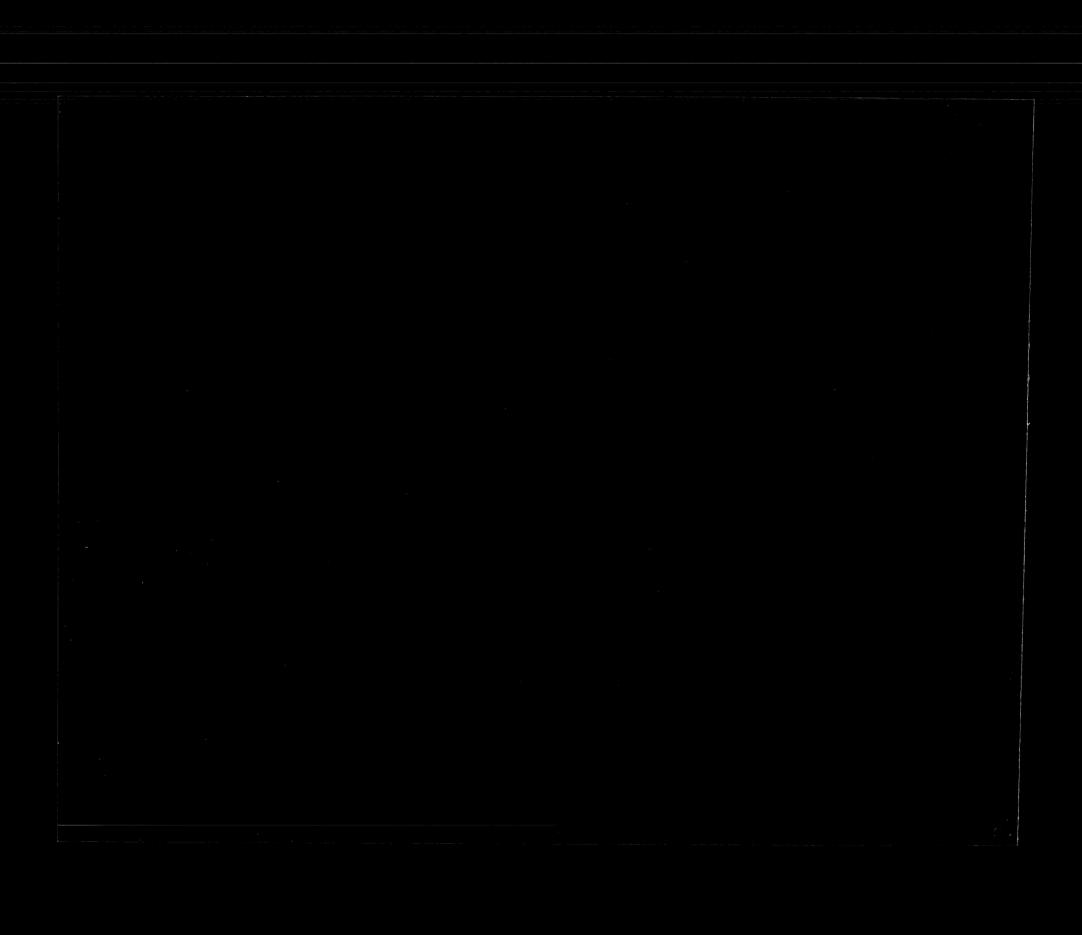

Kavarsk

Located 50 miles north of Vilna, the small town of Kavarsk, Lithuania, was founded in the 15th Century as the Estate of Pienionys. In the late 15th Century, the Grand Duke of Lithuania transferred the estate to Stanislovas Kovarskis. The first written reference to the town of Kavarskas occurred in 1538.

St. John the Baptist Church, constructed between 1857 and 1887,
mill pond in foreground
Kavarsk, Lithuania

"Fall has already arrived. The last bright days of the dying summer are getting cooler...The grains have already been harvested from the fields. The gardeners have already picked from the gardens...The birds have already flown away to warmer climes.

The winds and the rains are about to begin. And in the shtetl it is looking gloomy from all the muddiness. On the houses and in the streets and in the whole shtetl a depressed mood prevails. It is quiet all around...Winter is already approaching. And in this way everything comes to an end in the fall."

Market Day - Kavarsk, 1936
Monday was market day in Kavarsk.

Celebrating Lithuanian Independence Day, February 16, 1933
Lithuania proclaimed its independence from Russia in 1918.

Public gathering, date unknown

Krenitzeh, cold spring
A series of troughs funneled spring water to the roadside for drinking

Beile Delechky at the Krenitzeh

Enamel cups, attached to chains, were provided for drinking the spring water.

Kauno tunelis.

The Kovno Railway Tunnel linking Kovno and Vilna, completed in 1861
as part of the St. Petersburg - Warsaw Railway.

The first Jewish settlers arrived in Kavarsk at the end of the 18th Century. By the end of the 19th Century they numbered about 1,000 people working as business owners, craftsmen, farmers and peddlers.

The Russians deported the Jews to the Russian interior during World War I. At the conclusion of the war, about 100 families, roughly half of Kavarsk's Jews, returned to their homes.

Kavarsk had a Jewish population of approximately 500 in 1940. On September 5, 1941, the Jews of Kavarsk were murdered in the Pivonia Forest.

Jews and Christians

The Jewish Cemetery
Kavarsk

Michel Labe Segal
Beile Delechky's grandfather

Michel Labe had a little shop where he sold groceries, eggs, and produce, some of which he purchased from farmers. He also sold fruit that he harvested in his orchards. The store that Michel Labe owned did not prosper and he eventually gave it up.

Michel Labe was also a peddler, carrying goods on his back and selling them to neighboring villages and Vilna. He would go out, his big black coat filled with pins and needles. He would return at night with chickens in the pockets of his coat.

A prince owned the lands in the area where Michel Labe and his family lived. The fields and orchards were rented for the season by Jews as well as by non-Jews. Jews were not permitted to own land. The negotiations for rental took place during blossom time. An average orchard had about one hundred trees. The harvested fruit was shipped out by railroad to larger cities as well as being sold in local markets. Michel Labe rented an orchard and he and his family harvested and sold the fruit. During the summer the children would camp on the land to protect their crop from thieves and vandalism.

Michel Labe was a very religious man and a scholar. He studied at night and knew 24 Masechtot of Gemara. He taught Hebrew to his children and grandchildren and also had students from other families. He took over the rabbi's job when no rabbi was available.

In his old age, it became increasingly difficult for him to trudge off to the synagogue three times a day. Fruma, his youngest daughter, was unmarried. She took care of her father in his old age. With the money that her brothers from America sent her for a dowry, Fruma bought a piece of land and a house. There she and her father lived. She sold vegetables and he taught students.

Michel Labe was about 84 years old at his death in 1930. He predicted his own death. He put on his tallis and died during the night.

From 'The Siegel Family '80', a family history.

Here lies buried our Father,
the Learned and God Fearing
Michel Labe, Son of Chaim, who
departed in the year of 1930, in
the first day of Shivat.

May his Soul rest in Peace.

The Synagogue Dweller

So why are you wailing over the Talmud
Pale synagogue dweller?
My dear synagogue dweller
You and your wailful tune
My heart goes out to you

And my eyes became full
And with blood-shot tears
My dear synagogue dweller
Tell me what happened to you

Maybe you're pining away for them
For father, mother, sister, brother
To whom you have become
like a ship without a rudder

And maybe the whole day at Leiben's
You sat a whole day
Until he said, "You, young man.
Take the cup and wash your hands to eat."

And maybe you're simply a shy guy
Eating bread at strangers' tables
And with blood and hot tears
You scarf down every morsel

And you just remembered right now
And you can't stomach it
And by the Rebbe
You now want to wail your heart out

Well then, sing your tune even louder
Higher, louder, only then
Will your loneliness dissipate
And your hunger be sated

Catholic funeral service

Funeral procession

At School

Jewish elementary school (Folks-Shul) - Kavarsk, 1931
The schoolhouse included four rooms: two classrooms, a
recreation room and a teacher's living quarters

Class picture
February 15, 1927

Two teachers taught at the Jewish elementary
school.

One, employed by the government, taught Yiddish,
Lithuanian and the government-specified
curriculum.

The other, employed by the parents, taught Hebrew
and the Bible.

Staff of the children's library at the Kavarsk
Folks-Shul, 1926-1927
Beile Delechky top left

School report card (Lithuanian / Hebrew)

	חתימת המנהל / Vedėjo parašas	חתימת המדריך / Auklėtojo parašas	Nebuvo, kartų	Pavėliavo, kartų	Dėmesys	Stropumas	Elgesys	Dailraštis	Rankdarbis	Paišyba	Gimnastika	Dainavimas	Higiena	Istorija Bendroji	Istorija Lietuvos	Istorija Žydų	Geogr. Lietuvos	Geogr. Bendroji	Krašto moks.	Gamtos mokslas	Matema Geometrija	Matema Aritmetika	Žydų kal. Biblija	Žydų kal. Kalba	Lietuvių kalba	התרפ"_1_ / 192_5_
		—																								השליש הראשון / I trečmetis
		—																								השליש השני / II trečmetis
		—																								השליש השלישי / III trečmetis
	אהרן שור					5	5	5												3		4+	3	3	4	ציון שנתי / Metinė Žymė

החלטת המועצה הפדגוגית: להעביר למחלקה אלף

Pedagogų Tarybos nusprendimas: ....

.... **Vedėjas**

חתימת המנהל: ח. לוין

Left: Beile's report card for 1925/26 with grades for diligence, behavior, penmanship, science, arithmetic, Bible, the Prophets and Hebrew

Pažymėjimas.

Šiuo pažymima, kad *Beilę Seliačkaitė* iš *Kvarsko*

gim 19*14* m. *Rugsėjo* mėn. *9* d. *Kvarsko Ukmerges* apskrityje *Izraelitų* tikybos, įstojo 1923 m. *Rugsėjo* mėn. *1* d. į Ukmergės apskr. *Kvarsko* valsč. *Kvarsko Žydų* pradžios mokyklą, mokėsi joje visus *5* metus iki 19*28* m. *Birželio* mėn. *1* dien. šiu mokslo dalykų: tikybos, lietuvių kalbos, aritmetikos, gimtinės mokslo, krašto mokslo, gamtos mokslo, mankštybos ir žaidimų, geografijos, istorijos, dainavimo, grafikos ir dailyraščio ir šiais 192*8* metais baigė šios mokyklos kursą.

Mokslas buvo einamas prisilaikant Švetimo Ministerijos patvirtintosios 1925 m. spalių 25 d. pradžios mokykloms programos.

Komisija, duodama *Beilei Seliačkaitei* šį pažymėjimą, vadovavosi 192*7* —2*8* mokslo metų darbais ir egzaminų daviniais.

192*8* m. *Rugpiučio* mėn. *10* d.

Egzaminų Komisijos Pirmininkas,
Kvarsko Žydų **prad. mokyklos Vedėjas** *Ch. Grinas*

Kvarsko prad. mokykl. vedėja : *Tillinvegineij*
Valsč. akštoras : *M. Liber*
NARIAI *Teris komiteto.* : *M. Lurie*

Beile's primary school diploma August 10, 1928

Beile attended the school from September 1, 1923, to June 1, 1928. The curriculum consisted of religion, Lithuanian, arithmetic, homeland studies, local area studies, nature studies, physical education and exercise games, geography, history, singing, drawing and penmanship.

Children's plays

June 20, 1938

February 4, 1938

At Work

Kibbutz 'Matsref' [The Crucible], cutting lumber, Shaki, Lithuania
May 18, 1934

Beile milking a cow

In the apple orchard

The apple harvest
Beile, two unidentified men, Abraham and Minna Delechky

Lithuanian soldiers, 1937
The Lithuanian Army consisted of 24,000 men organized in three infantry
divisions. Much of its equipment was outdated.

When the Soviet Union annexed Lithuania in June 1940, the Lithuanian Army was absorbed into the
Red Army. Faced with the Nazi invasion of June 22, 1941, the Red Army withdrew from Lithuania.
German forces overran the country in three days.

Iron and Steel

What are you thinking about, my heart
My childish heart
It's high time, you wised up
It's time today
When everyone is hard
When birds and tigers are transformed

Today is the time for iron and steel
Do you hear that noise, that banging?
That is the heart
within its gigantic breast
Like a thief who wants to grab it all

You live at a time when everything is repressed
Love, feelings, tears
Only the hard metal prevails
And it oppresses
And refuses to soften

(The Last Sunday) Tango

Now is not the time
To look for a way out
When everything is already lost
Do you have a rich one? And he's the only one you love?
And so where should I go with you now?

I have just one plea
And maybe this is the last one
A plea of many years standing
Give me a Sunday
A Sunday, just one
And after that the world can go under

Friends

"...a bright whiteness shines through from the pure snow which is covering the earth. But then people pass by leaving behind black patches carved out by their footprints.

There is hope that the snow will come to an end. There is hope that once again we will behold the green grasses on which we can lie down and rest.

But the dawn arises again and the snow begins to tumble. More snow accompanies a swirling from the eternal wind. And you're praying and wondering, 'When will this bitter, cold, raging wind come to an end?'"

"…how sad it is in the forest. The trees stand enveloped in sadness, with their branches bent to the ground. The angry winter-wind lashes out in anger with its roaring voice.

But the branches, with their own strength, are able once again to let their heads rise up, and beseech the Lord to put an end to the angry winter.

…the young saplings stay dry and shake with their weak little heads, and contemplate and ask: How much longer will the winter with its angry wind prevail?

The terrible winter will pass. There will once again be life, these trees are murmuring. But nearby there are prideful pines with their elegance, as if to say, 'Look at our green garments; they haven't fallen off; we are always nice and green. We are graced by God.' And one imagines that a silent voice is ringing in the forest. God will be for everyone…"

Friends at the Pintiker Rock
July 15, 1938

"...the Pintiker Rock. This rock looked like a very, very big loaf of bread...lying there half into the ground... hunched over, probably from "old age,"...

Faigeh had a camera. When the sun sent off its last rays we ...posed by the rock. (I did too.) But on our card the stone was tilted because of Faigeh's constant high spirits."

"The whole purpose of our excursion was to meet new friends and create a Chalutzish [Zionist pioneers] camp environment.

The Chalutzim all around were making a tumult, making noises, joyful and singing... Many had themselves photographed. Photos for mementos...

We also had a 'collective snack', and a little girl sang for us some beautiful songs in Russian, Hebrew and in Yiddish.

After all the boisterousness in this Chalutz atmosphere, and tanned from the sun's rays--we took a breather and started

"Several Zionist pioneers accompanied us ...for the return trip. All of these comrades had come to have fun in the forest somewhere near a large and stubborn rock. There were eighteen of us. We were being boisterous, singing and making merry as much as we could get away with. With me, occasionally, there were times when I called it a day. I would suddenly become extremely introspective... The heart was grieving but didn't know why.

It didn't take us long to get to the river. From there, we had to be rowed across. This was by the Feslaer Mill. So we all paused and called out to the other bank. A bright gray mist spread out over the nearby fields of green. The day, in the meantime, was dying off. The sun, big and round, was moribund in the west and lit the heavens with streaks of flaming red. ... The air was mild and comfortable, but the impatience that called us home began to make its demands --"What are we standing around for? We need to paddle across!" It was getting dark; the comrades were starting to complain. "Why did we need to go home so late? Now we're going to have to wait half the night!" The boat was berthed by the edge of the water, not far from the rapids and waiting for an experienced boatman to navigate the treacherous water. Unfortunately, there were no experienced rowers among us. We started hollering across to the other shore. A Christian person came and informed us that we would have to wait fifteen minutes until three stars begin to parade across the heavens; and only then would the proprietor take us across.

So our "captain" spoke up with a proposal: "What are we waiting for?--in the meantime let's start sailing." We jumped into the boat in pairs. When the boat started to depart, my sister jumped in and called out, "Comrades, with a "captain" like this we will all soon drown." She was thinking of her two brothers and myself, foreseeing the possibility of a catastrophe... Our "captain" was very confused. Seeing the rapids like an enraged animal close by , he started sailing the boat to open water in terror that he couldn't overcome the infuriated waves. He threw the rudder into the water, and lightening fast we were in the rapids. The water made stormy, boisterous sounds, like a wild enraged creature which was ready to swallow up everything. That little area where the water was raging, boiling, looked like hell. At the shore stood eight men who were waiting until the boat would return and take them across. They were screaming frantically. All that screaming was causing us to be even more confused. My older brother was holding the boat in check by grasping at the rudder. Two boys jumped into the water and swam to the shore, and made it safely across. The panic was great. The "screamers" just made things even more tumultuous. The remaining people in the boat started jumping into the water, recklessly, not aware of where they were. But sensing danger in the boat, they thought that swimming would save them. Faye jumped into the rapids and yelled out, "Jump into the water. Let's swim!!" The camera that she had carried with her she threw onto the river bank and called out that it should be given to her sister.

The "captain" instantly jumped into the water, followed by my younger brother. For a moment they were both submerged but both managed to surface again. I became frozen from fright. I grabbed the "captain" by his jacket, but he slipped through my hands. I grabbed his hand and he quickly dragged me into the water. I yelled for help and Ly Piniankeh ran to the edge of the boat and helped me drag the "captain" from the water. At that moment I noticed a head ...sliding away from the foamy waves. I felt that this was truly a crisis. This was my brother! I grabbed him by his jacket and I started dragging him with all my strength. With one hand I was holding him and with the other I was holding the captain. I was overcome with fear. I felt like I was going to faint. I was feeling so terrible, I was struggling to hang on with my last bit of strength. L.P. was holding on to the "captain" with both hands. For me to drag my brother--I had no strength. I took water from the river and I splashed myself. Things were getting better; I was coming to. Ly and I got down to business pulling in the two wet "warriors." We were barely able to pull them in. They were heavy, very heavy, from being wet. Momentum aided the process. When they finally got into the boat, I stood there for a while completely in a daze. Only a little bit later did I come to. I looked around and I saw my sister and cousin dragging Faye out of the water. In my state of confusion I had no idea where she had ended up. I had thought she was still on the boat. I couldn't figure out what the most critical thing was to do. I had to take care of business wherever I found it.

Suddenly, another boat with the proprietor appeared on the scene. He arrived at the behest of the "screamers." This proprietor was our savior. He called out, "Take a head count! Are all of you here?" One by one we jumped from our boat into the rescue-boat. Why was everyone jumping around like this?--he couldn't understand the insanity of jumping. He was angry, his hands were shaking. Nothing was in order. Faye had jumped in and was completely drenched from her "swimming." Seeing that everyone was in the boat and secure, a couple of kids started laughing. Faye was also giggling. I told her to turn aside so that the proprietor would not recognize her. Everyone was very disturbed and confused. The proprietor was still looking very pale, not used to this type of disturbance. It brought out his rage and hatred of Jews.

Once we got to the shore we had to somehow manage. The "drowned" ones were drenched through and through.

We started heading for the road, with the knowledge that after this near disaster everyone had something to talk about. It was already nighttime and getting dark. The croaking of frogs wafted in the air. A cacophony of bird chirpings came from somewhere, as if from a great, great distance. The forest was now behind us. Everywhere surrounding us were fields spread out and bathed in fresh dew. A blue sky and bright dotted stars sparkled over our heads. All this looked to me like a fantastic legend out of some myth. It seemed as if absolutely nothing had happened. We had made it all up. Presently, the mild summer air was caressing all of us. The sound of the dresses as the wet girls walked mixed with the croaking of the frogs and chirping of the birds, a sound pounding out like a melody from Nature's Orchestra.

I couldn't help sinking into thought. Many thoughts cropped up, about doom and existence, about suffering and ephemeral freedom, from fleeting success to perennial suffering. All these things, all these things, came up in my thoughts.

We made a racket, we ranted and bantered on about how all this had taken place. It was a conquest over the powers of nature. We had risen above it. Everyone was keen to get their version across. I wanted to put things off for later. Stories were told. There was ranting going on. Others, still in a state of terror, couldn't even begin to describe what had happened to them. I caught the mood of this whole bunch. I wanted to distract myself from it all. I went over to one of the "screamers" and we composed a mourner's march. As we continued on our way back, I came to realize that this was a disparate group; everyone felt separate from the rest. It was now pitch-dark. It was chilly and everyone was tired. We were all wet; and feeling the cold in our wet clothing, we needed to speed up our walking.

The night frost did more than a little to goad us on, and very quickly we arrived at the shtetl. We came marching in, joyful and lively, as if from an "excursion." We parted company with each other, little by little. When parting, we wished each other a speedy recovery in a very warm bath. One woman we passed along the way picked up on our salutations, which piqued her interest. She asked, "what was at the bottom of your going into the pitch darkness? What was there to see ?" " Ah, nothing!" And I shot back for everyone: " There was no bottom. If only there had been a bottom!" A couple of people understood and started laughing loudly. The woman was bemused. A bunch of us began parting company, and we wished each other a speedy recovery."

Yokeh, Beile's best friend
July 25, 1934

Yokeh survived the war, emigrating to Israel. She and
Beile corresponded but never saw each other after 1938

```
|                 |         |              |                    |          |        |
Pearl  M.  Yankel Berman   Raisel   Channa  M.  Chaim Favin   Minna  M.  Faivel Chaet   Abraham   Beile   Moishe
         |
   ————————————
                                              |
   |      |       |                         Liebe
Raisel  Yitzahk  Vichke
```

The Delechky Family

The Delechky family home and small general store

Back Row - Channa, Raisel, Beile, Minna, Abraham.
Seated - Pearl, Raisel, Chaya, Rafael, Yankel, Yitzahk.
Front - Moishe

Chaya and Rafael Delechky with their grandchildren,
Yitzahk and Raisel Berman, and Liebe Favin

Chaya Rachel Delechky

Moishe, Minna, Abraham, their mother Chaya
and niece Raisel

Moishe, Beile, Minna, Raisel and Abraham

Moishe

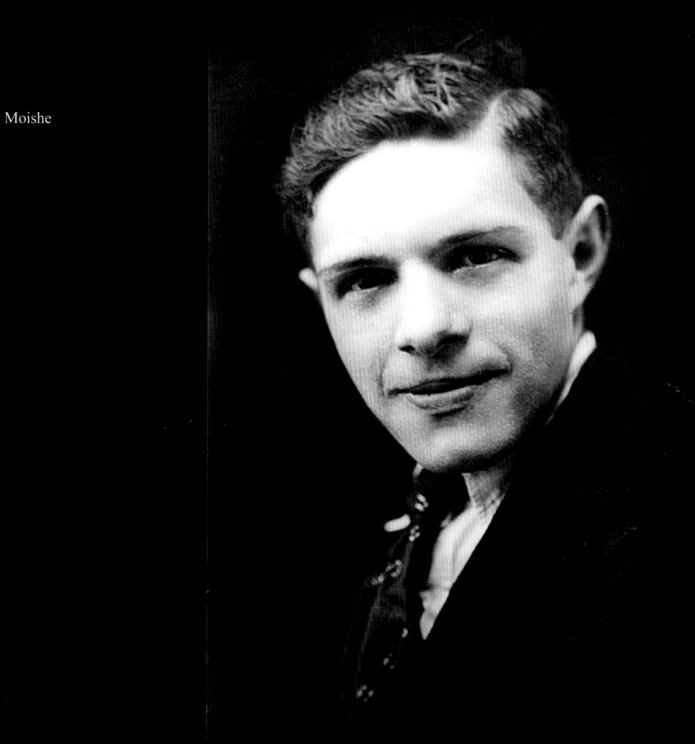

Moishe in the Lithuanian Army
1939

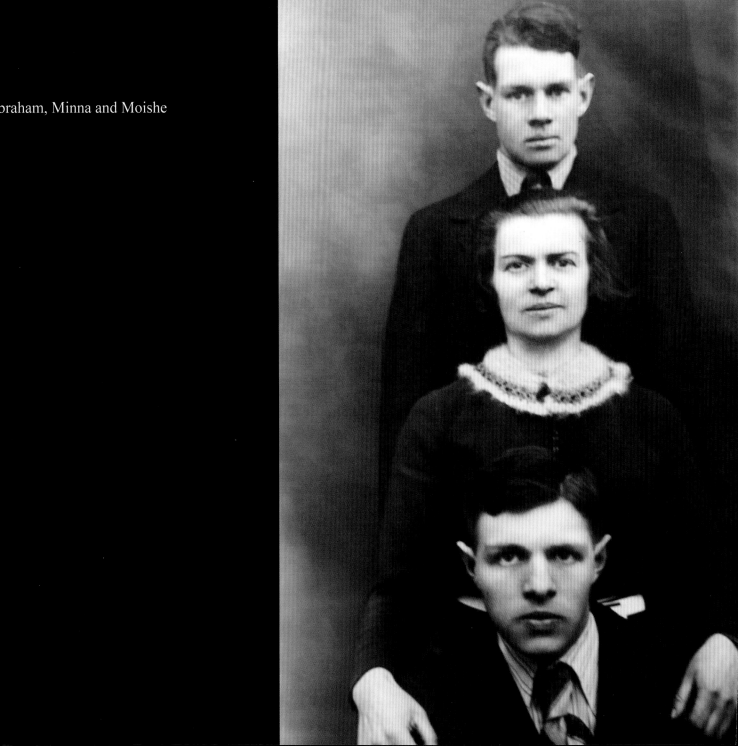

Abraham, Minna and Moishe

Moishe and Liebe
1938

Pearl Delechky

Pearl, Raisel and Yankel Berman
June 8, 1932

Pearl, Raisel, Yankel and infant Yitzahk

Liebe, Abraham, Yitzahk, Pearl, Yankel and Raisel

Channa Delechky
1931

Chaim, Liebe and
Channa Favin
July 25, 1936

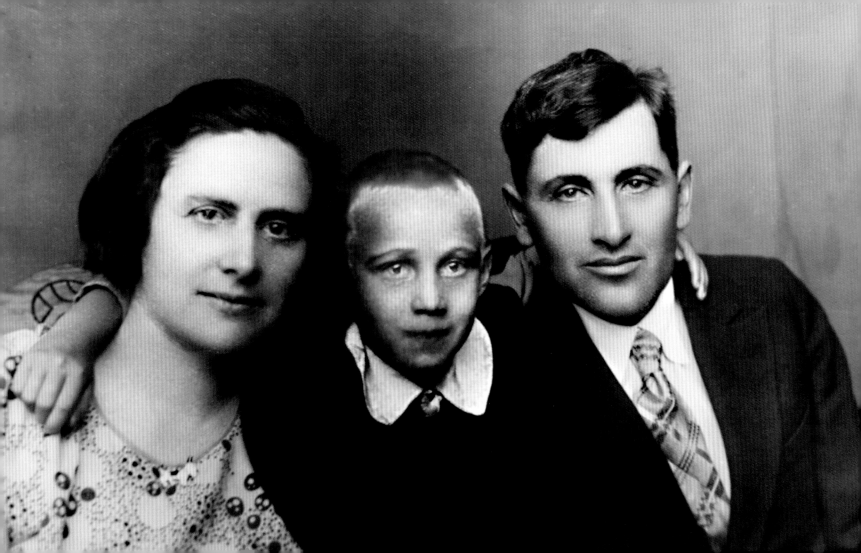

A Little Rain

Children, oh children, a little rain
Quite wonderful, fragrant raindrops
A little rain is God's grace,
Come on out and dance around
With bare feet and heads
Thinking about nothing, asking about nothing
Children grow in the rain
Bare heads, bare feet.
Every child will grow to become a giant
And reach up to the sky

Yitzahk Berman
1937

Liebe Favin

Raisel Berman and
her Aunt Beile

Raisel Delechky

Raisel married and emigrated to Argentina before the war. She and her husband Noah raised a son and two daughters.

Raisel and Beile were reunited in 1976 when Beile visited Buenos Aires.

Raisel and Faigeh,
Yokeh's sister
1932

Raisel and Beile

Minna Delechky
September 18, 1934

A member of the Communist Party, Minna Delechky was
a partisan during the war, fighting against the Germans
and their Lithuanian allies. She was wounded in combat
but survived the war.

After the war, Minna and her husband Faivel lived in
Vilna, raising a daughter. Minna and Beile corresponded
regularly but never saw each other after 1938. Minna died
in 1980.

Minna and her mother
September 1939

Beile and Minna
May 22, 1938

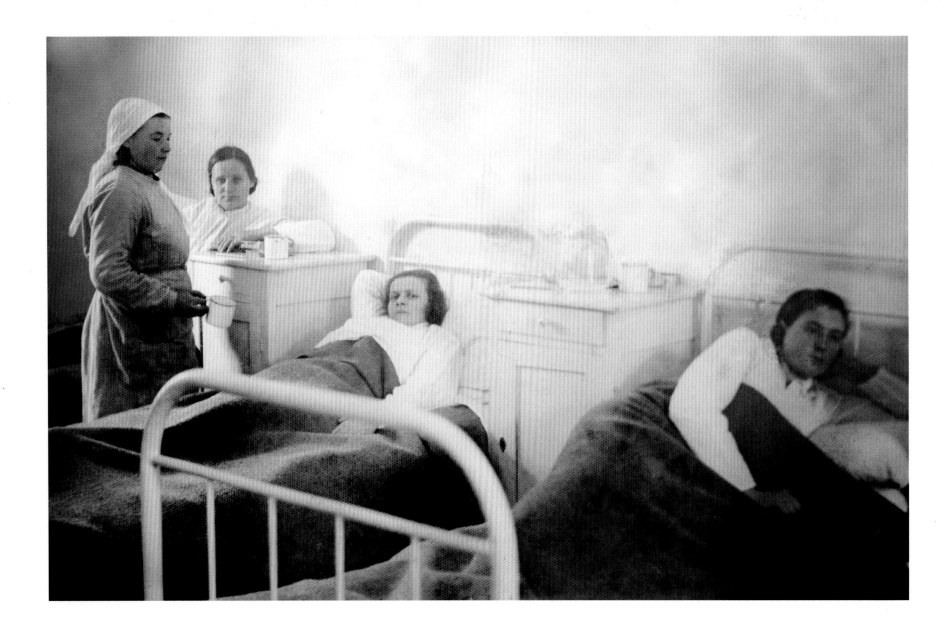

Minna and Faivel Chaet
March 20, 1943

Beile and Minna
1938

Opposite:
Beile Delechky

Liudijimas.

Kavarskas,1937 mt.vasario m.19 d.Mes,žemiau pasirašę
1)L u r i j a,Mauša,Joselio sūn.,2) Z i s k i n d a s ,Izra-
ėlis,Iciko sūn.ir 3) P a n o v k a,Elija,Chackelio sūn.,visi
gyven.Kavarsko miestely,liudijame,kad D i l i a č k a i t ė,
Beilė,Rafaelio duktė,gyvenanti Kavarsko miest.,Kavarsko valsč
tikrai yra gimusi /1914/ tūkstantis devyni šimtai keturiolik-
tais metais gegužės mėnesį,Kavarsko miestely,Kavarsko valsč.

Šį liudijimą tvirtiname savo parašais ir už jo tikrumą
atsakome visais savo turtais einant įsttymu.-

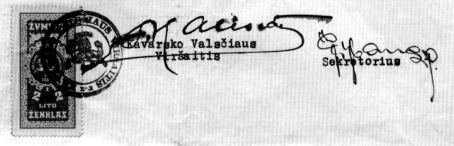

Savarankiškus parašus liudininkų : Lurijo,Maušo,Jose-
lio sūn.,Ziskindo,Izraėlio,Iciko sūn.ir Panovkos,Elijo,Chac-
kelio sūn.,gyvenančių Kavarsko miest.,Kavarsko valsčiaus sa-
vivaldybė tvirtina savo parašais ir antspauda.-

m.Kavarskas,1937 mt.vasario m.19 d.Ns.488

Kavarsko Valsčiaus
Viršaitis

Sekretorius

A certificate signed February 19, 1937, giving 1914 as Beile's birth year. Her passport states 1912. In her journals, she gives her birth year as 1918.

When a Friend Only Asks

You ask me, my friend
How old am I today?
I would have no hesitation to tell you
But believe me, my friend
I myself don't know
Because I haven't given thought to keeping count

A tightwad counts money on a successful day
One that loves a fortune and dearly
My life, my friend, is
A long desolate road
And just as in years past
So it is today

If life means suffering
Then I've been living a long life
Then I've lived to a ripe old age
If life means hearing of joy
If it is only a sound
Then I haven't even been born yet

Beile and her
cousin Helena

Beile and
Moishe Delechky
displaying their
photography

1938

Beile Delechky
1938

1933

June 16, 1938

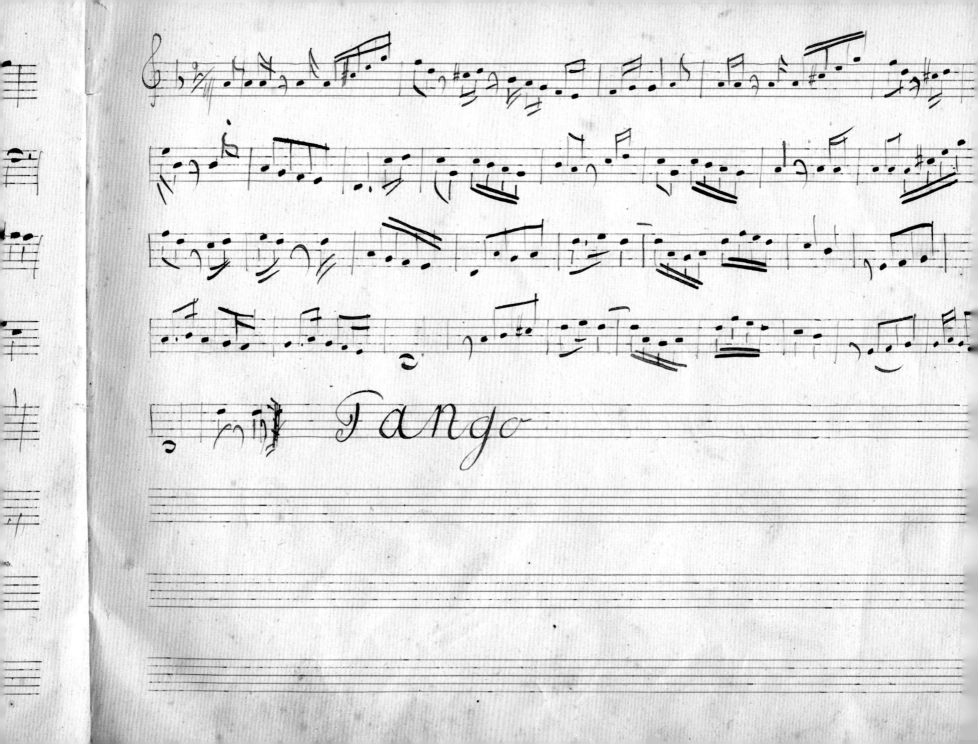

Tango

Beile's violin music

Beile Delechky

My low laced boots
In the rain
Why do you let me hear
The drops on the windows

And the boots are torn
And the streets are getting muddy
Very soon the winter will arrive
And I don't have a warm, long coat

My low laced boots
The candle which you let me hear
It melts and it drips its tallow
And it will soon be extinguished

In this way, I thank you
Like a candle weak and dark
Until I will be extinguished
Quietly, in the eastern corner

My low laced boots
The watch that you let me hear ticking
With its yellow numerals
With its ringing and its chimes

It's like an empty vessel
It is lifeless, without emotions
When the hour arrives, it must strike
Without any desire, without any will

My low laced boots
This life which you permit me to hear
Lazy, wilting in my youth
Prematurely aging

Begging food, pouring out tears
Sleeping on a hard bench
Dying in This World
And waiting for The World to Come

To America

Visa from the U.S. Consulate allowing Beile's immigration to the United States

Kaunas, Lithuania
September 3, 1938

Under the Immigration Law of 1924, only 150,000 immigrants were allowed entry into the U.S. each year. That number was divided among national quotas based on the proportion of each nationality in the U.S. population in 1920. The annual quota for Lithuania was 386.

Amerikos Konsulatas

Pųtvinskio gatvė 42, Kaunas, ... Sep. 3, 1938
(Data)

Gerbiamasis ar Gerbiamoji:

B. Diliačkaitė, Kaunas, Kęstučio gt. 41/16

(Vardas-pavardė ir adresas turi būti įrašyti imigranto)

Jūs esate užregistruotas .... Lietuvos .... kvotos laukiamajame sąraše, ir šiuomi pranešama Jums, kad kiek galima spręsti prieš Jūsų atvykimą atrodo, kad dokumentai, kuriuos Jūs pristatėte įrodymui, kad jei įleistas į Jungtines Valstybes Jūs negalėsite pasidaryti visuomenės našta kada nors ateityje, yra patenkinami, ir Jūs turite atvykti

1938 m. spalių mėn. 5 d. iki 11 val. ryto padaryti formalų prašymą vizai gauti. Vienok, reikia pridurti, kad negalima Jums duoti užtikrinimo, kad viza bus Jums išduota iki Jūs neateisite asmeniškai į Konsulatą, būsite fiziniai apžiūrėtas vieno iš žemiau išvardintų gydytojų (kuriam tikslui išsimaudykite ir pasiruoškite), ir kitaip patikrintas, su savo dokumentais, ir būsite pripažintas turinčiu teisę gauti vizą pagal Amerikos imigracijos įstatymų ir taisyklių.

Toliau perspėju Jus, kad jei neatvyksite į Konsulatą patikrinimui viršnurodytą dieną, Jums, gal būt, reikės gauti naujus arba papildomus dokumentus garantuojančius Jūsų išlaikymą Jungtinėse Valstybėse sąryšy su galinčiais įvykti aplinkybių pakeitimu Jūsų byloje.

Asmenys priklausantieji ne prie Lietuvos, bet prie kitos kvotos (kas liečia daugumą asmenų gimusių ne Lietuvoje), jei jie po jų atvykimo ir patikrinimo buvo pripažinti turinčiais teisę į vizą, turės laukti iki Konsulatas galės išgauti jiems vizos numerį iš atitinkamo Kvotos Kontrolės Valdininko tame krašte, kur jie gimė. Kiek laiko tai gali užimti, negalima pasakyti iki atitinkamas Kvotos Kontrolės Valdininkas nebuvo prašytas Konsulato prisiųsti numerį, ir atsakymas gautas.

Pirmiau negu atvykti į Konsulatą viršnurodytą datą, Jūs **turite** atvykti 9 val. ryto tą pačią dieną arba pas Dr. S. Laurinavičių, Putvinskio gatvė 30, arba Dr. Ch. Finkelšteiną, Mickevičiaus gatvė 31 abudu Kaune, fiziniam apžiūrėjimui. Pilna kaina už fizinį apžiūrėjimą yra 5 litų, kuriuos Jūs turite apmokėti patys. Ateinant į Konsulatą Jūs turėsite pristatyti Medicinišką Liudymą dublikate, kurį daktarai išduos Jums po mediciniško apžiūrėjimo.

Asmeniški dokumentai surašyti kitoje pusėje šio lapo irgi **turi būti** Jūsų išgauti ir asmeniškai pristatyti šiam Konsulatui atvykstant viršnurodytą dieną ir laiku. Jei dėl kurios nors priežasties Jūs negalite išgauti kurio nors dokumento, reikalinga tuoj apie tai pranešti Konsulatui laišku.

PASTABA: Atvykstant į Konsulatą **turite** atsinešti su savimi šį pranešimą, Jūsų tapatybės nustatymui ir šiuomi Jums pranešama, kad imigrantų vardai, neatvykusių paskirtą dieną, išbraukiami iš laukiančių sąrašo.

Su tikra pagarba

už Konsulą

Walter J. Linthicum

Amerikos Vice Konsulas

"The 9th of November, 7 o'clock in the evening. Riding out of Kaunas. A historic day for me. A dream is coming true. Emigrating and to where? - to America. Only six months ago this seemed like an illusion. Yes, an utter illusion…

Everything inside me feels feverish, soul, blood - everything…I have no strength even to place one foot forward. Nevertheless, I'm racing around. I'm not running, I'm flying like a butterfly in spring. My soul is very much at ease, but deep inside, deep inside, my soul is smoldering…

And what will I be expecting next? I don't know…I'll have to start from scratch again."

"The train is blowing the signal. I bid farewell to all. A whole bunch of people have come out to say goodbye. With what kinds of feelings, I have no idea. All I know is that I'm off to America.

The clerk at the counter is directing me to the train. Here, in just a moment, I am inside. I stand next to the window and I shake a handkerchief. They do the same. Everyone is escorting me, waving their hands."

ŽYMĖS
SIGNALEMENT

Žmona — Épouse

Žmona — Épouse.

Užsiėmimas
Profession
{ fotografė
photographe

Gimimo vieta
ir laikas
Lieu et date de
naissance
{ Ukmergės aps.
Kavarskio m.
1912-V-3 d.

Nuolat. gyvena-
moji vieta
Domicile
{ Ukmergės aps.
Kavarsko m.

Šeimos padėtis
État civil
{ netekėjusi - célibataire

Veidas
Visage
{ pailgas - oblong

Akių spalva
Couleur des yeux
{ pilka - gris

Plaukų spalva
Coul. des cheveux
{ šviesi - blond

Ypat. žymės
Signes particul.
{

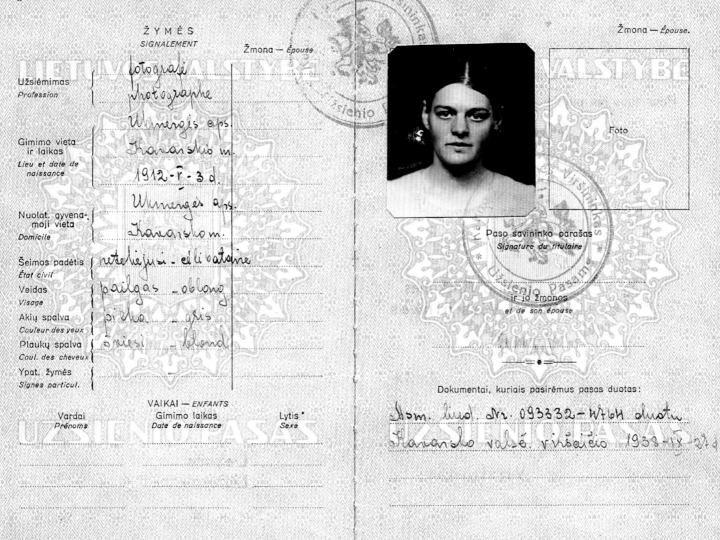

Foto

Paso savininko parašas
Signature du titulaire

ir jo žmonos
et de son épouse

VAIKAI — ENFANTS

Vardai Prénoms	Gimimo laikas Date de naissance	Lytis Sexe

Dokumentai, kuriais pasirėmus pasas duotas:

Asm. liud. Nr. 093332-W764 duotas
Kavarsko valsč. viršaičio 1938-IX-27d.

Beile's Lithuanian passport
Beile passed through Nazi Germany, entering on November 9, 1938, and crossing into Holland on November 10,

Diliaekaite Beile

LIETUVOS VALSTYB

VIZA Nr. 3600

Tinka keliauti _viena_ kartą
iš Lietuvos pro bet kurią val-
džios nu statytą sienos peržengimo
v ą į _Amerika_
nuo dienos išdavimo iki
1939 m. _sausio_ mén. 13 d.
Kaunas, 1938 m. _spalių_ m. 14 d.

Kauno Apskrities
Viršininkas

SIENIO PASAS

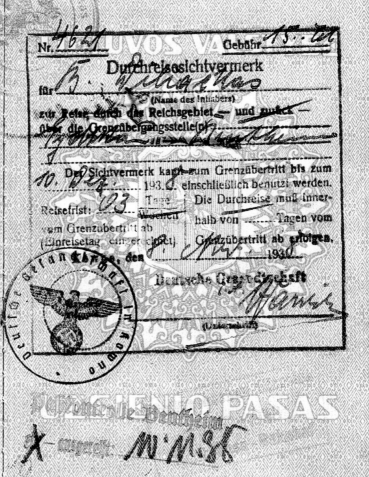

Nr. 4624   Gebühr 15 tr

Durchreisesichtvermerk

für B. Diliaekas
(Name des Inhabers)

zur Reise durch das Reichsgebiet — und zurück —
über die Grenzübergangsstelle(n)

Der Sichtvermerk kann zum Grenzübertritt bis zum
193 . einschließlich benutzt werden.

Reisefrist: 03   Tage   Die Durchreise muß inner-
Wochen   halb von — Tagen vom
vom Grenzübertritt ab   Grenzübertritt ab erfolgen.
(Einreisetag einger chn t)

Kaunas, den   1938

Deutsche Gesandtschaft

(Unterschrift)

PICHIENIO PASAS

Over the night of November 9 and 10, 1938, the Nazis orchestrated riots throughout Germany aimed at synagogues and
Jewish businesses. Twenty six thousand Jews were arrested and sent to concentration camps. Ninety one died during the riots
From the smashed windows of Jewish businesses, homes and synagogues came the name given to this pogrom, _Kristallnacht_

"(In Amsterdam) the hotel guy, a young man…, a Dutchman who speaks German, leads me to the bed chamber. Up, up the staircase-where did they come up with so many stairs? They're endless. The feet are getting weighed down and the steps seem interminable. I ask him if there are also steps in Rotterdam. He says to me in German with a smile: 'Wherever there are great obstacles, there you will find many steps.' And I am thinking that it was made especially for such (an) emigrant."

"On the way, I find myself socializing with three decent German women. During the entire trip they talked about nothing else but food, florid dresses and dogs.

We come to Rotterdam and everywhere they speak Germanized-Dutch. One gets the impression that outside Lithuania there is nothing but Germans. The Jews are all so Germanized, it's hard to recognize them. They all sprechen Deutsch."

"On Friday evening, the 11th of November, 1938, I have had the fortune to take my first steps towards going to America. It's 8 PM in the tourist hall. Here they formalize the papers and they let many passengers through. It's a long staircase that extends from the tourist hall all the way to the ship deck. A young man is approaching me and I go with him. He…escorts me up the stairs taking the first steps to America!

All around from the distance, the fires of Rotterdam are sparkling, millions of fires with reflections in the water. It's a wonderful sight…Escorts are gathering. We see this from a distance. We're getting ready to leave."

Holland-America Line. t.s.s. **VEENDAM.** 15450 tons register - 25620 tons displacement

The ship that brought Beile to America
November 1938
Beile spent 12 seasick days crossing the stormy North Atlantic.

"And my dear mother, my good-hearted mother, I left her alone. The parting has been very difficult. My mother is standing next to my bed; I imagine her here in the hotel with tears in her eyes. And she is pleading, 'Beilkeleh, please don't leave me alone, I'm pining away for you, who will look out for me?'

(I) just lie there with my eyes closed and think into the distant, into the distant future which still hasn't materialized. Will these new friends be good to me? Will they feel like the old ones? Like the family that is there forever?"

"On the tenth, I arrived in Berlin, and the same evening to Holland, Amsterdam. On the eleventh of November I arrived in Rotterdam. The next day, all day, I was occupied dealing with the papers in Rotterdam. On the same day that I celebrated, I took a ship and we were off for America.

On the 23rd, I'm at the New York harbor ceremonies disembarking from the ship. I spend a little time in New York and then, on the same day, I catch a train to Chicago. I arrive in Chicago on the 24th, 25th, on the 26th after time in Duluth, on to Virginia (Minnesota)."

Beile's Yiddish poetry

Following page: English translation

Black Eyes

Eyes black, dreamy and large
Glances deep, haughty and hot
Eyes black, full of sorrow
As if they regret that love and success don't last
forever
Yes, success!

Yes! Why remind oneself and grieve?
And why not be able to have everything?
That in any event everything is lost
The lustfulness of those years
It will never again come back,
Yes, back!

I will no longer be kissing you, my beloved
I will no longer be loving you, sad one
Like a dream that flew away
Your deep black eyes
Like a dream of love, and of success
Yes, success!

Eyes black, full of intensity
You still mesmerize me, just as you always had
Night after night you soar over me
The past speeds by faster and faster
Steals my sleep and steals my time

Oh, night, your duration is like eternity
I see, I see, those eyes of yours
They are the same pleading eyes
Why have you deserted me?

The morning arrives and I hope
When will my suffering come to an end?
And as soon as I go out into the street
Again, I see your eyes piercing me like an arrow

I see, I hear, something from the past
And I hear from a distance your lovely voice
I see, but see those eyes of yours
They are the same pleading eyes
Oh, why have you deserted me?

An American citizen, May 19, 1944

I Believe and Hope Today for a New Beginning

I believe and hope for a new beginning.
Because old folks avoid joy
Because all my limbs are exhausted
For new joys, a new song

Today I'm afraid of who I am
Because it's difficult to go against yourself
Still I need partner time today
And to be prepared for the coming struggle

For a new world, a new path
For a new time, a new god
For free thought in a free world
And hope never absent

This, my goal, the past to exchange
For all free world ways
For borrowed joy when in pain
To seek joy--not to avoid it.

When she passed through Ellis Island, Beile Delechky was given the name Betty Del.

She lived two and a half years in the small town of Virginia, Minnesota, staying with her Aunt Jennie, her mother's sister. She worked in the family store and went to school to learn English and study for citizenship.

Betty moved on to Cleveland, Ohio, staying with her relatives, Blanche and Max. There she worked for five and a half years at the Majestic clothing factory, attended night school and sang in Jewish night clubs. She took the oath of citizenship in Cleveland in 1944.

In 1947, Betty traveled to San Francisco to visit a girl friend from Cleveland. Instead of staying for two weeks, she stayed for the rest of her life. She married, and with her husband, Arthur, raised a son and two daughters. Betty never forgot her home and family in Lithuania and never stopped grieving for their loss. But she took pride and happiness from the home and family she made in America.

Beile Delechky
1918 - 2002